STRANGE WORLDS

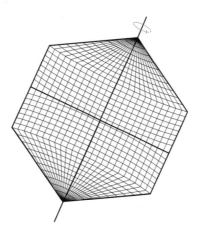

Lazy Dog Press

MATTHEW ALBANESE

MATTHEW ALBANESE

STRANGE WORLDS

with an essay by
DAVID REVERE MCFADDEN

Lazy Dog Press

CONTENTS

THE INWARD EYE

DAVID REVERE MCFADDEN

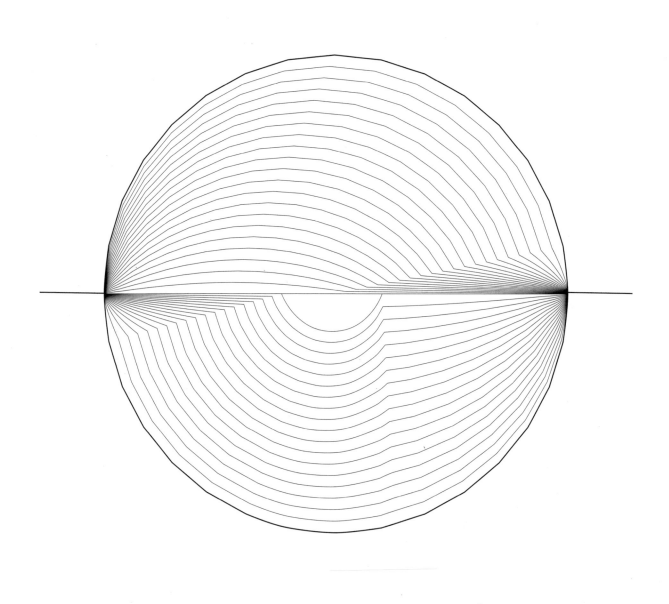

The poet *William Wordsworth wrote about his "inward eye," which served him like a camera, making it possible to resurrect in his mind, "a host, of golden daffodils; beside the lake, beneath the trees." Matthew Albanese's strange worlds, captured in radiant color images, are also brought back to life by way of the artist's inner vision. These are worlds that seduce the viewer into believing that the forests and lakes, waterfalls and glowing nighttime auroras, the windswept savannahs, the jewel-like coral reefs, and even the surfaces of distant moons and planets are photographically accurate documents of specific environments. It is only when one learns that these natural phenomena are constructed of the most banal and quotidian of materials—spices, bottle brushes, salt, fake fur, and deconstructed feather dusters—and that they are only as large as a small tabletop, that the viewer becomes aware of having been gently persuaded and then seduced into believing in a reality that is entirely false. Rather than feeling cheated, deceived, and manipulated by the artist's clever wiles, a strange pleasure, sometimes approaching awe, kicks in, taking the viewer into the state of suspended disbelief that we experience at the theater or in the movies.*

Born in 1983 as an only child in his family, Albanese learned at an early age the value of solitary play and invention. His reticent manner and his modesty today are clearly reflections of this background. He went on to study photography at the State University of New York, Purchase, and received his Bachelor of Fine Arts degree in photography. Making photographs has been the artist's occupation ever since; but the photographs with which he earned his living were, until he began to focus more and more of his time and talent on making independent art works, commercial in nature—retail, architectural interiors, and fashion. While an accomplished technician with the camera, Albanese has always been more interdisciplinary in his studies, combining photography with sculpture and color theory, both of which were to play critical roles in the development of his unique oeuvre.

Albanese's world is Janus-faced, one aspect presenting the world in its idyllic splendor, and the other revealing a much darker side. The seemingly pristine beauty of the natural world in Waterglass Mountains *is bathed in atmospheric light; tall trees embrace a pristine lake, while in the distant background snow-capped mountains rise magnificently into a cloudless azure sky. Simulations of water particularly intrigue the artist, and offer him the opportunity to transform humble props into convincing simulations of reality. In this vista and in* D.I.Y. Paradise *—a sun-filled tropical landscape with billowing white clouds over a turquoise sea—there is an ironic "picture postcard" quality to the image, the artist's wry acknowledgment of the falsity of the world that this clever artist-cum-travel agent has created. Albanese has created other vast panoramas that range from a wind-swept prairie in* After the Storm *to the drama and visionary quality of the Northern lights in* Aurora Borealis. *In every image, however, the artist has left clues as to the true identity of the materials that comprise the stage sets for his photographs. Trees begin* to reveal themselves to be scouring pads and brushes, lush cumulus clouds turn out to be drugstore cotton balls, and the gentle lapping waves of the ocean are seen as food-color tinted boiled sugar poured over crumpled aluminum foil.

This inviting and gentle tweaking of nature stands in contrast to another series of works that explore the more menacing and even hostile world of destruction and angst. One recent work, A New Life, expresses the duality of the world in Albanese's mind. The focal point of the artist's diorama used to create this two-part photograph is a venerable weeping willow tree (made from hand-dyed ostrich feather down originally used as a feather duster) that grows at the edge of a stream or watery estuary. The artist uses this setting to create two distinctly different photographic images. One version situates the scene at sunset; the glowing remains of the setting sun produces apricot, pink, and tangerine streaks in the billowing clouds and on the gently rippling surface of the water. In the other version the very same props become the players in a much more unsettling drama: grey storm clouds block the sky, while the willow, *so gently passive in the other image, looks ancient and frail as it is blown by a cold and unrelenting wind. The viewer is caught between the seductive poetry of the sunset and the harsh reality of the impending storm.*

The works in this series are embodiments of the Jungian shadow we strive to repress. Albanese's often chilling revelations of the dark side of the world (and, hence, our lives) have the same magnetic power that forces us to stare at disasters, whether natural or man-made. Tornado *places the hapless viewer in the direct path of the tempest. Immanent destruction is also implied in* Breaking Point, *a violently erupting mountainous volcano. While we can take some comfort in the fact that these natural phenomena are beyond any human control and not subject to our intervention, there are other works that place the responsibility for destruction more clearly in human hands. While the raging flames in* Wildfire *may have been generated by a lightning strike, they may also be the result of human carelessness or malevolence.* Burning Room *is equally ambivalent in its essence: a comfortable domestic interior is being consumed* before our eyes by searing flames that appear to have specific locations in the upholstered furniture, carpet, and drapes, suggesting arson rather than accident. Even more disturbing is the chaotic horror depicted in Train Wreck, one of the artist's more recent works. Strewn over the landscape are the shards and remnants of a train, punctuated by a massive column of fire exploding in the distance. The chilling aspects of Albanese's scenes are underscored by the complete absence of any human figures.

It is the pervasive sense of isolation and helplessness in the face of these destructive forces and action that gives Albanese's photographs their memorable power. Isolation in a world without apparent order, a world of illusion and deception, suggests that the artist's aim is not to entertain us with his clever wizardry in creating these scenes, but rather to pose moral questions of belief, identity, and meaning in our relationships with the natural world.

Probably nowhere is this feeling of isolation and helplessness more profoundly described than in the artist's visions of worlds far removed from human intervention.

In both Everything We Ever Were, *which positions the viewer on the surface of the moon, and in the artist's earliest work* Paprika Mars, *the atmosphere of loneliness and longing is nearly palpable.*

Matthew Albanese's worlds, whether superficially gentle or blatantly violent, place the viewer in an existential quandary. Are we the anonymous and blameless witnesses to a world of deception that both entices and mocks us? Are we asked by the artist to enter a territory entirely fabricated in the artist's mind or does our suspension of disbelief override our knowledge of what is true and what is false? In permitting ourselves to become a part of the artist's world, are we reading his own autobiographical narrative? Which is the human presence we recognize in these landscapes?

Carl Jung wrote that our "projections change the world into the replica of one's own unknown face." *Matthew Albanese's strange worlds serve two masters: they are projections of the artist's unknown face, but also of our own.*

STRANGE WORLDS

MATTHEW ALBANESE

A New Life #1 — *BACKSTAGE 68, 69*

A New Life #2 — *BACKSTAGE 68, 69*

Above the B.Q.E.

After the Storm — *BACKSTAGE 70*

Aurora Borealis — *BACKSTAGE 71*

Burning Room — *BACKSTAGE 76*

How to Breathe Underwater — BACKSTAGE 74, 75

D.I.Y. Paradise — *BACKSTAGE 80, 81*

Paprika Mars #2, #1 — *BACKSTAGE 91*

Salt Falls — BACKSTAGE 82

Tornado — BACKSTAGE 83

Train Wreck — *BACKSTAGE 84, 85*

Wildfire — BACKSTAGE 88, 89

My Dream, Your Nightmare — BACKSTAGE 90, 91

TESTS

*My work uses exacting
technique, but the technical aspects
are merely a means.*

*I'm far more interested
in sharing concepts, themes, and
emotions than fixating on the work's
nuts and bolts.*

REEF TEST

—

This is a test for *How To Breathe Underwater*.
The purpose of this was to determine how well the
materials and lighting would work together.
The lighting was achieved using six different
strobes, various filters, and a video projection.
The challenge was in applying this to a larger scale.
The coral is made out of wire, tulle, beads, cast wax,
jelly beans, fabric glitter, preserved starfish, and
walnuts. Despite how well the fan coral turned out,
I wasn't able to work it into the final composition.

LIVING ROOM TEST

—

This model took one month to plan,
acquire components, and build only
to be destroyed in fifteen minutes.
It was one of my favorite models to
construct and to destroy.

WILLOW STUDY

—

For *A New Life* I first created the willow tree
that was to become the main subject of the
work. I was confident that the materials I was
using would work, but I was unsure how to scale
the tree itself and how to layer the sections of
feathers in a believable way.
Unlike the tree in Willow Study, I wanted it to
feel large and majestic. Once I completed the
study I understood that I had to rethink my
approach. I ended up stripping the framework
of the tree bare and recreated it layer by layer
until I was absolutely satisfied.

FOREST DETAIL

—

This was a very basic test in which
I was focusing on the depth of field.
The materials themselves are very small
and I wanted to see how far I could push
them. The test didn't materialize into
anything specific, but I did reference
the composition of this work in
My Dream, Your Nightmare.

The test shots I take for a new landscape I am about to create forces me to approach my work from a more technical point of view. Since each new work can now take up to seven months to complete, testing allows me to verify whether or not my newly developed techniques and strategies will be successful. It's about making a strong commitment to the work in an environment that lends itself to experimentation through making mistakes. It's in making wrong turns that my greatest discoveries are made.

Much to my surprise, the paint on the parchment paper was all I needed.

The mistake had transformed the parchment paper into the river I was searching for.

When I was testing for *A New Life* I had decided that I would use cooked sugar to create the river, it was just a matter of getting the color right. I laid down parchment paper and painted it a muddy brown, the perfect color. But as the paint began to dry on the paper it warped, crinkled, and bubbled up and I thought I would have to rip it all up and start again, which often happens. Much to my surprise, the paint on the parchment paper was all I needed. The mistake had transformed the parchment paper into the river I was searching for.

The moon test was a way for me to experiment with rear projection. It allowed me to repurpose a failed test for the planet Mars. By stripping the color out I was able to transform it into the moon. The moon test is really a projected photograph within a photograph. I wanted to see how effective projection would be and also to learn the best way to capture this type of image. This is actually a test for a work I have not yet approached.

For the moon I was inspired by the lyrics:

PALM STUDY

—

The purpose of this test was to determine how well the turkey feathers would function as palm trees. To do this quickly I shot them in silhouette. It was a very basic maneuver of aiming a spot light onto a white canvas creating the illusion of a burning tropical sunset. Once I saw that the outline of the feathers worked well, I moved on to the more meticulous and time-consuming process of painting and detailing the palm trees.

BILLIONS & BILLIONS

—

I created this to test for the star field in *Aurora Borealis*. I was interested in the concept of dramatically altering an object by the simple act of puncturing holes in it in a very haphazard, free-form manner and then blasting light through the holes to create an endless space. A boring cork board that I used to hang annoying bills and daily reminders on became a piece of infinity.

"I miss you like the stars miss the sun."

MOON TEST

—

Made from bottle brushes, black paper, video projection, spattered phosphorescent ink.

earth	⬡		**TOOLS:**	work boards	spotlights	tripods	computer
meridian	‖‖			canvas roll background		reflex camera	work table
parallels	≡			paint brushes	pots	time	light bulbs

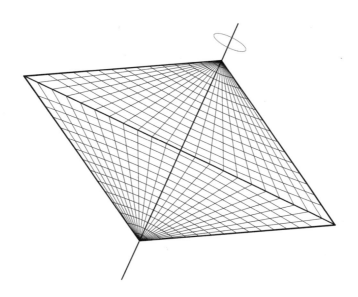

BACKSTAGE

Behind the scenes of **STRANGE WORLDS**

PAGES · 32 — PICTURES · 63   **TYPE** · *DTL Fleischmann · Verlag*   **PAPERS** · *Sappi GalerieArt Volume 150 gsm ·*
· Fedrigoni Freelife Vellum White 120 gsm ·

I create small-scale handmade dioramas out of everyday, mundane materials which, through the lens of my camera and the use of lighting, are transformed into hyper-realistic images. In my worlds ostrich feathers turn into willow trees, steel wool morphs into a tornado, cooked sugar assumes the form of a glacier, and paprika makes up the surface of mars. Nothing is off limits. Each diorama can take up to seven months to build, light and photograph.

I often discover by chance new methods and techniques which I then try to implement into future work. I'm deeply influenced by the world of special effects in film; I treat each diorama as if it were a miniature movie set, a small film still of a place that exists for a short period of time before gravity sets in. The final photograph is always the final destination of a deeply emotional and creative journey.

A New Life

link *p.*18—19

I had originally intended to do only one piece for *A New Life*, the one with the sunset, but as I was making the willow tree I noticed how my breathing was having a strong effect of motion on the feathers. So I decided I would try to work that sense of wind sweeping through the tree. I kept bouncing back and forth between the two and then it dawned on me that I could just do both. I think these two works demonstrate how important the actual photography is to my process.

The lighting, the colors and the special effects play the most important roles in producing the final work.

wire	painted parchment paper	thread	hand-dyed ostrich feathers	raffia
ELEMENTS				
synthetic potting moss	coffee	masking tape	carved chocolate	cotton

After the Storm

link *P.*23

ELEMENTS	faux fur
sifted tile grout	*cotton*

Aurora Borealis

link *p.*24—25

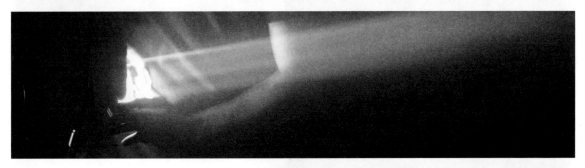

I am inspired by many things:
song lyrics, poetry, film, specifically
the making of and behind-the-scenes
aspects. I am especially drawn to
science fiction, not only because of the
fantastic places and characters that the
genre produces but also for the sheer
magnitude of visual effects that are
usually required to bring them to life.

A MIXTURE OF MANY DIFFERENT ELEMENTS	
strobe light	cork board
a beam of colored light	
real leaves	black curtain

Breaking Point

link P.27—29

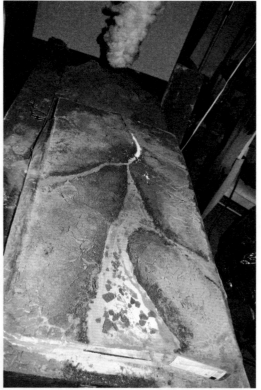

ELEMENTS	
tile grout built on a sheet of glass	
cotton	*6 60-watt light bulbs*

How to Breathe Underwater

link *P.*32—33

This was an extremely difficult build.
As the miniature was not physically shot
underwater the greatest challenge was
making it appear as if it were. In order to
do this I first had to find materials that
exhibited the proper qualities of how

the objects they represented reacted to light. The best example of this would be the sea anemones which were made out of jelly beans and had the perfect variation in color and translucent properties. It took three weeks just to slice them open, roll them into shapes, and then assemble them. In order to light the piece as if it were underwater, I consulted an avid diver and asked what it is like down there. The most valuable advice was that the red spectrum of light becomes muted the further down you go. To achieve this, I covered my lens with a piece of blue stretch wrap thus finding the right balance of reds to greens and blues. In order to recreate the rippling effect of sunlight shining down in rays, I created many different patterns of black-and-white squiggles and lines in a Photoshop image which I then projected (using a video projector) onto the diorama bathing the elements in the foreground with a "diffracted" light. In this work, by far the most complex lighting scenario, I used a total of 11 different light sources.

clear epoxy		poured and cast candle wax		walnuts	sponges
figs	plaster	wax coated seashells	clay	Q-tips	nonpareils
ELEMENTS					
wire	feathers	vinyl shower curtain	compressed moss	Plexiglas	toothpaste
peanut shells		dyed starfish	flock	glitter	jelly beans

Burning Room

link *P.*30—31

Burning Room came about at a time in my life in which I needed greater independence. I was living at home during this period and desperately desired to be self-sufficient and on my own. Since burning down my actual home was not an option, I modeled the room after the living room in my house in order to watch it burn. I had created something that resonated with the deep burning desires I have for wanting something better, something more, the fire as a total catharsis. *Burning Room* is the only diorama I had to actually set ablaze in order to fully realize the final shot. It was a risk and I love taking risks, but this is where testing comes in very handy. I tested the shot sequence a dozen times before I was confident that I could get the shots I needed. Many of my dioramas get a bit messed up during the shoot; it's just a matter of cleaning up a mess and resetting it from the beginning. For example, each sequence of shots for *Salt Water Falls* resulted in a large pile of salt in the focal point of the image. I just had to keep cleaning the salt, adding the details back in and doing it over and over again until the waterfall revealed itself. It

can be very nerve wracking and tedious at times, but it's also what makes the process so exciting.

ELEMENTS				
wood	purchased dollhouse furniture	nylon	Plexiglas	fire

Everything We Ever Were

link *P.*51—53

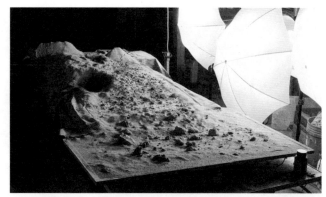

It took two months to store up enough fireplace ash to create this lunar landscape. The title of this work was one of the few that came before the image. I was always enamored with the Earthrise photograph taken during the Apollo 8 mission. It was the first time the Earth was portrayed as an isolated ball of blue floating in space, the first time we could see our entire planet and thus humanity as a whole.

ELEMENTS		
ash	crumpled paper	mixed tile grout
video still projection		wire

Icebreaker

link *P.*35

Three days of cooking,
and two weeks of building.

ELEMENTS						
25 pounds of sugar cooked at varying temperatures (hard crack and pulled sugar recipes)						*powdered sugar*
salt	*egg whites*	*flour*	*corn syrup*	*cream of tartar*	*India ink*	*blue food coloring*

D.I.Y. Paradise

link *p.*36—37

People are always shocked to see how low-tech my dioramas are. To the naked eye they don't look anything like the final image which is 90% photography and 10% construction.

ELEMENTS	feathers	canvas
	tin foil	salt
	cotton	cooked sugar

The photography is the most rewarding and exciting part of my process. This is when the world I have created comes alive, the walls of my studio fall away, and I feel as if I am actually "there."

Salt Falls

link *p.*40—41

I consider the photographs I produce (and not the small-scale models) as the works themselves, but I have no problem revealing my work process. I think it excites people to see how the photographs were made. When I was young I was absolutely obsessed with special effects and movie magic. Instead of focusing on the film, I would observe and learn all of the fascinating and unexpected ways filmmakers would solve visual problems and bring the extraordinary to life in a convincing manner. Whenever an adult would ask me what I wanted to be when I grew up, I would always reply that I wanted to make special effects for movies!

ELEMENTS	painted canvas	tile grout	dry ice	twigs	glass
	falling table salt		Plexiglas	moss	salt

Tornado

link *P.*42—43

It took three months to create the tornado out of steel wool. I created three different incarnations of the actual twister until I found something that worked well with the materials. Though it isn't evident when looking at the final piece, steel wool is very messy and unforgiving!

ELEMENTS	steel wool	moss
	cotton	ground parsley

Train Wreck

link *p.* 44—45

Fire represents very different things in my work. A loss of control, a clearing or a cleansing, strong desires (which relates more to *Burning Room*). I light my miniatures to reflect different times of the day in order to build greater context into the work. I like that the images often look like they could be a film still. I also like focusing on fine details and, at times, leave hints that they are fake: "telltale signs" such as the hard edge on the ball of fire in *Train Wreck*. I find it interesting when viewers look for the flaws and can actually find them. It's sort of a suspension of disbelief that occurs; in one moment it looks like a real place, then suddenly it looks fake, and then back again to "reality."

I chose the subject of a train wreck for its idiomatic usage. We often say: "That person is a total train wreck." The moment you receive bad news that alters your life you might say your life has been "derailed," which was the emotion I was drawing on for this work.

electrostatic grass	pine brooms	airbrushed Plexiglas	wood	umbrella parts	cat litter
ELEMENTS					
watch and music box components		Lionel train cars		cotton	orange and red party bulbs

Waterglass Mountains

link *p.*47

In this photograph it was the discovery
of the material, which happened by
chance, that informed the work. It was
a quiet summer evening and I was having
dinner with a friend on the patio on one
of those outdoor "waterglass" tables.

tile grout	painted canvas
ELEMENTS	
bottle brushes	moss

The only source of illumination was from the tealight candles resting directly on the surface of the table. I immediately took notice of the properties of the glass. Our quiet dinner dissolved away as I became transfixed on the lake which the surface of this table would later become. I built my next strange world right there on the patio table. It wasn't so much something I had to create as much as discover. This one is more about seeing than making.

Wildfire

link *p.*48—49

In the beginning I chose to create disasters to convey an even greater sense of scale. It's one thing to create a calm or barren sweeping landscape out of fur or sugar, but to recreate natural phenomena of dangerous and destructive magnitude such as an erupting volcano or a dark muscular tornado out of innocuous material like steel wool contributes to a sense of awe.

Even the works I create that are not based on some sort of destruction have a very unsettling quality. In most cases there is a lack of any human presence, no sign of animal life, no birds in my skies, no fish in my reef. I am most excited by a work when I feel as if my eyes are the first human eyes to fall on any particular place or event, a sort of quiet empty space that exists in the first moments of discovery, a solitary meditation that is equally beautiful as it is dark. *Wildfire* was the result of a technical progression in making fire. I decided that I was not yet satisfied with how I was creating my fire effects and wanted to essentially turn up the heat. I felt the need to clear my mind and my creative space and what could do that more effectively than a forest fire?

ELEMENTS					
Scotch-Brite pot scrubbers		*clipping from a bush in bloom*			*wire*
paper	*clear garbage bags*	*wood*	*yellow, red, and orange party bulbs*		*moss*
yellow glitter	*clear thread*	*cooked sugar*	*sand*	*tile grout*	*bottle brushes*

My Dream Your Nightmare

link *P.*54—55

If I am uninspired I will sometimes go "shopping" for inspiration. I'll look at window displays or fabric stores, I especially like the grocery store. I'm always searching for a material that jumps out at me, and then ask myself, "Hmmm, what could that be?"

synthetic electrostatic grass		spattered phosphorescent ink		watercolors
ELEMENTS				
artist charcoal	sticks	crepe paper party streamers		sifted coffee

Paprika Mars

link *p.*38—39

I think my work has matured a great deal since my first piece, *Paprika Mars*.
Not only have I perfected the technical aspects such as the building of the miniatures and the forcing of the perspective, but the photography has improved as well. I am now much more comfortable going to whatever place I need to emotionally. I no longer hesitate about putting my raw emotions into my work for everyone to see. Each piece represents a specific time, place, or event in my life. I have found the more deeply inspired I am, the more powerful the work becomes.

ELEMENTS		
chili powder		paprika
thyme	cinnamon	charcoal

32-33 · 48-49 **GLITTER** *How to Breathe Underwater, Wildfire*						

Elements

| **51-53**
CRUMPLED PAPER

Everything We Ever Were | **48-49**
CLEAR THREAD

Wildfire | **54-55**
WATER COLORS

My Dream, Your Nightmare | | **38-39**
THYME

Paprika Mars | **35**
FLOUR

Icebreaker | **38-39**
CINNAMON

Paprika Mars | **38-39**
CHILI POWDER

Paprika Mars |

| **35**
INDIA INK

Icebreaker | **54-55**
CREPE PAPER PARTY STREAMERS

My Dream, Your Nightmare | **54-55**
STICKS

My Dream, Your Nightmare | **32-33**
NONPAREILS

How to Breathe Underwater | **42-43**
GROUND PARSLEY

Tornado | **32-33**
FIGS

How to Breathe Underwater | **35 · 36-37 · 48-49**
COOKED SUGAR

Icebreaker, D.I.Y. Paradise, Wildfire | **35**
CREAM OF TARTAR

Icebreaker |

| **18-19 · 48-49 · 51-53**
PAPER

A New Life, Wildfire, Everything We Ever Were | **24-25**
BLACK CURTAIN

Aurora Borealis | **18-19**
THREAD

A New Life | **42-43**
STEEL WOOL

Tornado | **32-33**
WALNUTS

How to Breathe Underwater | **18-19**
HAND-DYED OSTRICH FEATHERS

A New Life | **18-19**
CARVED CHOCOLATE

A New Life | **35 · 36-37 · 40-**
SALT

Icebreaker, D.I.Y. Paradise, Salt Falls |

| **36-37 · 40-41 · 47**
CANVAS

Paradise, Salt Falls, Waterglass Mountains | **32-33**
CLEAR EPOXY

How to Breathe Underwater | **24-25**
A BEAM OF COLORED LIGHT

Aurora Borealis | **24-25**
CORK BOARD

Aurora Borealis | **35-36-37**
BLUE FOOD COLORING

D.I.Y. Paradise, Icebreaker | **32-33**
PEANUT SHELLS

How to Breathe Underwater | | |

| **20-21 · 32-33**
PLASTER

Above the B.Q.E., How to Breathe Underwater | **40-41**
TWIGS

Salt Falls | **18-19 · 32-33 48-49 · 51-53**
WIRE
A New Life, How to Breathe Underwater, Wildfire, Everything We Ever Were | **27-29 · 90**
PHOSPHO-RESCENT INK

Breaking Point, My Dream, Your Nightmare | | | | **30-31**
FIRE

Burning Room |

| **30-31**
NYLON

Burning Room | **36-37**
TIN FOIL

D.I.Y. Paradise | **30-31 · 32-33 40-41 · 44-45**
PLEXIGLAS
Burning Room, How to Breathe Underwater, Salt Falls, Train Wreck | **32-33**
Q-TIPS

How to Breathe Underwater | **18-19**
SYNTHETIC POTTING MOSS

A New Life | **27-29 · 82**
MODEL MADE OUT OF GLASS

Breaking Point, Salt Falls | **44-45 · 54-55**
ELECTRO-STATIC GRASS

Train Wreck, My Dream, Your Nightmare | |

| | | | | **44-45 · 48-49**
PARTY BULBS

Train Wreck, Wildfire | **48-49**
WHITE FLOWERS

Wildfire | **18-19 · 23 · 27-29 36-37 · 42-43 · 44-**
COTTON
A New Life, After the Storm, Breaking Point, D.I.Y. Paradise, Tornado, Train Wreck | |

The Periodic Table

of STRANGE WORLDS

48-49 — SCOTCH-BRITE POT SCRUBBERS — *Wildfire*

32-33 — VINYL SHOWER CURTAIN — *How to Breathe Underwater*

51-53 — VIDEO STILL PROJECTION — *Everything We Ever Were*

18-19 — MASKING TAPE — *A New Life*

27-29 — PHOSPHOROUS INK — *Breaking Point*

27-29 · 40-41 · 47 · 48-49 · 51-53 — TILE GROUT — *Breaking Point, Salt Falls, Waterglass Mountains, Wildfire, Everything We Ever Were*

Food

5 — POWDERED SUGAR — *Icebreaker*

35 — EGG WHITES — *Icebreaker*

32-33 — JELLY BEANS — *How to Breathe Underwater*

8-39 — PAPRIKA — *Paprika Mars*

18-19 · 54-55 — COFFEE — *A New Life, My Dream, Your Nightmare*

35 — CORN SYRUP — *Icebreaker*

24-25 — STROBE LIGHT — *Aurora Borealis*

32-33 — TOOTHPASTE — *How to Breathe Underwater*

47 · 48-49 — BOTTLE BRUSHES — *Waterglass Mountains, Wildfire*

44-45 — UMBRELLA PARTS — *Train Wreck*

44-45 — WATCH — *Train Wreck*

44-45 — LIONEL TRAIN CARS — *Train Wreck*

44-45 — CAT LITTER — *Train Wreck*

32-33 — CAST CANDLE WAX — *How to Breathe Underwater*

44-45 — MUSIC BOX COMPONENTS — *Train Wreck*

23 — FAUX FUR — *After the Storm*

48-49 — CLEAR GARBAGE BAGS — *Wildfire*

27-29 — 6 60-WATT LIGHT BULBS — *Breaking Point*

30-31 — DOLLHOUSE FURNITURE — *Burning Room*

Tools

0-31 · 44-45 · 48-49 — WOOD — *Burning Room, Train Wreck, Wildfire*

18-19 — RAFFIA — *A New Life*

32-33 — WAX COATED SEASHELLS — *How to Breathe Underwater*

Natural elements

32-33 — DYED STARFISH — *How to Breathe Underwater*

32-33 — FLOCK — *How to Breathe Underwater*

19 · 82 — DRY ICE — *A New Life #2, Salt Falls*

32-33 · 40-41 · 42-43 · 47 · 48-49 — MOSS — *How to Breathe Underwater, Salt Falls, Tornado, Waterglass Mountains*

24-25 — LEAF — *Aurora Borealis*

48-49 — SAND — *Wildfire*

32-33 — CLAY — *How to Breathe Underwater*

32-33 · 36-37 — FEATHERS — *How to Breathe Underwater, D.I.Y. Paradise*

51-53 — ASH — *Everything We Ever Were*

44-45 — PINE BROOMS — *Train Wreck*

38-39 · 54-55 — CHARCOAL — *Paprika Mars, My Dream, Your Nightmare*

32-33 — SPONGES — *How to Breathe Underwater*

David Revere McFadden

is Chief Curator and Vice President for Programs
and Collections at the Museum of Arts & Design in
New York City. He served as Curator of Decorative
Arts and Assistant Director for Collections and
Research at Cooper-Hewitt, National Design
Museum, Smithsonian Institution from 1978 to
1995. For six years, he served as President of the
International Council of Museums' Decorative Arts
and Design Committee. McFadden has organized
more than 120 exhibitions on decorative arts,
design, and craft, covering developments from
the ancient world to the present day, has published
more than 100 catalogues, essays, articles, and
reviews, and has lectured extensively. McFadden
has received the Presidential Design Award three
times and has been named Knight First
Class, Order of the Lion of Finland; Knight
Commander, Order of the Northern Star
of Sweden; and Chevalier de l'Ordre des Arts
et des Lettres of France.

Matthew Albanese

Matthew Albanese's fascination with film, special effects and magic—and the mechanics behind these illusions—began early. Born in northern New Jersey in 1983, Albanese spent a peripatetic childhood moving between New Jersey and upstate New York. An only child, Albanese enjoyed imaginative, solitary play. He loved miniatures and created scenarios intricately set with household objects and his extensive collection of action figures. After earning a Bachelor of Fine Arts degree in Photography at the State University of New York, Purchase, Albanese worked as a fashion photographer, training his lens on bags, designer shoes and accessories—this small-object specialization is known in the retail trade as "table top photography." Albanese's creative eye soon turned to tabletop sets of a more wildly eclectic nature. In 2008, a spilled canister of paprika inspired him to create his first mini Mars landscape. More minute dioramas—made of spices, food and found objects—followed. In 2011, Albanese was invited to show at the Museum of Art and Design of New York. His work has also been exhibited at the Virginia Museum of Contemporary Art, Winkleman Gallery, and Muba, Tourcoing France. He is represented by Bonni Benrubi Gallery in New York.

lazy dog

LAZY DOG PRESS S.R.L.

HEAD OFFICE
Via Zumbini, 29
20143 Milano, Italy

ADMINISTRATION
Via Olmo, 45/B
37141 Verona, Italy

www.lazydog.eu

ALL WORKS BY · Matthew Albanese

DESIGN & ART DIRECTION · Massimo Pitis

EDITED BY
Debbie Bibo

GRAPHIC DESIGN · Elisabetta Calabritto

COLOR SEPARATIONS BY
Trifolio s.r.l.
using their extended
gamut system AREAW4

PRINTING AND BINDING · Trifolio s.r.l., Italy

TYPESET IN:
Verlag
DTL Fleischmann

PRINTED ON:
Sappi GalerieArt Volume 150 gsm
Fedrigoni Freelife Vellum 120 gsm

© 2013 Lazy Dog Press s.r.l., Milano

ISBN: 978-88-98030-03-3

First published in September 2013 — Printed in Italy